LIFE
of
ST. COLUMBAN.

LIFE OF
ST. COLUMBAN
BY THE MONK JONAS

EDITED BY
DANA CARLETON MUNRO

Reprinted by
LLANERCH PUBLISHERS,
FELINFACH, 1993.

ISBN 1 897853 03 3

FIRST PUBLISHED IN 1895 (PHILADELPHIA)
AS VOL. II, No. 7 TRANSLATIONS AND REPRINTS
FROM THE ORIGINAL SOURCES OF
EUROPEAN HISTORY.

LIFE OF ST. COLUMBAN, BY THE MONK, JONAS.

INTRODUCTION

During the sixth and seventh centuries the greatest missionary activity was shown by the Scots, who dwelt in Ireland. In that country religion was cherished with greater zeal than elsewhere, and learning was fostered for the sake of the church. But not content with the flourishing state of Christianity in their own island, the most zealous monks often passed over to the continent. There most of the inhabitants were still pagans, and the so-called Christians were little inclined to follow the precepts of the religion, which they professed. Gaul especially attracted the attention of the bold missionaries from Ireland, and the Irish usages became well established in some parts of the country. Unfortunately almost all the accounts of the missionaries from Ireland have been lost. But for this one biography, we could form no adequate conception of what the continent owed to them.

Jonas, the author of this life, became a monk at Bobbio, in Northern Italy, three years after Columban's death. He was soon employed to write this life, for which he obtained material, as he himself tells us, from the stories told by the saint's companions. Living as he did, among the latter, his account reflects their feelings faithfully, and we may be certain that he has recorded the events accurately, and has often reproduced the saint's own words. As is usual in such biographies, the miracles are numerous. For the contemporaries these formed the most valuable portions. For us, too, they are full of instruction, and throw much light on the daily life of the monks.

The language of Jonas is almost classical. But, unfortunately, he had little of the classical feeling for purity of style, and his writings are bombastic in the extreme. It is difficult to put his Latin into English. In some cases, I have been unable to determine the exact connection of some clauses with the context - if they have any. In such sentences I have translated literally, hoping that others might see a connection which I missed. In general, where I suspected a mistake, I have followed the Latin closely. A new and careful collation and transcription of the manuscripts would undoubtedly remove many of the difficulties.

I think there has been no translation of this life in any language before, except a very imperfect rendering of selected passages by Abel in the *"Geschichtschreiber der deutschen Vorzeit."* In this translation I have omitted from lack of space, the preface which has little or no importance for the life of the saint. All the rest is translated in full.

In this introduction, I refrain purposely from giving any summary of the saint's life, or even dates. Such statements here would lessen the value of the pamphlet for pedagogical purposes. With the single exception of the date of Columban's death, all statements can be interpreted by the data in the biography itself. On the other hand, I have generally modernized the names of places, because many of our readers who live far from large libraries, might otherwise lose the geographical information given here. The double purpose of our series renders such compromises inevitable.

THE LIFE
OF ST. COLUMBAN.

BY THE MONK JONAS

Migne: *Patrilogiae latinae cursus completus,* Vol. 87, cols 1014–1046. Latin.

6. St Columban, who is also called Columba, was born on the island of Ireland. This is situated in the extreme ocean and, according to common report, is charming, productive of various nations and undisturbed by contests with other peoples. Here lives the race of the Scots, who, although they lack the laws of the other nations, flourish in the doctrine of Christian strength, and exceed in faith all the neighbouring tribes. Columban was born amid the beginnings of that race's faith, in order that the religion, which in part that race cherished uncompromisingly, might be increased by his own fruitful toil and the protecting care of his associates.

But what happened before his birth, before he saw the light of this world must not be passed over in silence. For when his mother, after having conceived, was bearing him in her womb, suddenly in a tempestuous night, while she was buried in sleep, she saw the sun rise from her bosom and issuing forth resplendent, furnish great light to the world. After she had arisen from sleep and Aurora had driven away the dark shadows from the world, she began to think earnestly of these matters, joyfully and wisely weighing the import of so great a vision; and she sought an increase of consolation from such of her neighbours as were learned, asking that with wise hearts they should examine carefully the meaning of so great a vision. At length she was told by those who had wisely considered the matter, that she was carrying in her womb a man of remarkable genius, who would provide what would be useful for her own salvation and that of her neighbours.

After the mother learned this she watched over him with so great care that she would scarcely entrust him even to his nearest relatives. So the life of the boy aspired to the cultivation of good works under the leadership of Christ, without whom no good work is done. Nor without reason had the mother seen the shining sun proceed from her bosom, the sun which shines brightly in the members of the church, the mother of all, like a glowing Phoebus. As the Lord says: "Then shall the righteous shine forth as the sun in the kingdom of their father." So Deborah, with the voice of prayer, formerly spoke to the Lord, by the admonition of the Holy Spirit, saying: "But let them that love Thee be as the sun when he goeth forth in his might."

For the milky way in the heavens, although it is itself bright, is rendered more beautiful by the presence of the other stars; just as the daylight , increased by the splendour of Phoebus, shines more benignantly upon the world. So the body of the church, enriched by the splendour of its Founder, is augmented by the hosts of saints and is made resplendent by religion and learning, so that those who come after draw profit from the concourse of the learned. And just as the sun or moon and all the stars ennoble the day and night by their refulgence, so the merits of the holy priests increase the glory of the church.

7. When Columban's childhood was over and he became older, he began to devote himself enthusiastically to the pursuit of grammar and the sciences, and studied with fruitful zeal all through his boyhood and youth, until he became a man. But, as his fine figure, his splendid colour, and his noble manliness made him beloved by all, the old enemy began finally to turn his deadly weapons upon him, in order to catch in his nets this youth, whom he saw growing so rapidly in grace. And he aroused against him the lust of lascivious maidens, especially of those whose fine figure and superficial beauty are wont to enkindle mad desires in the minds of wretched men.

But when that excellent soldier saw that he was surrounded on all sides by so deadly weapons, and perceived the cunning and shrewdness of the enemy who was fighting against him, and that by an act of human frailty, he might quickly fall into the precipice and be destroyed, - as Livy says, "No one is rendered so sacred by religion, no one is so guarded, that lust is unable to prevail against him," - holding in his left hand the shield of the Gospel and bearing in his right hand the two-edged sword, he prepared to advance and attack the hostile lines threatening him. He feared lest, ensnared by the lusts of the world, he should in vain

have spent so much labour on grammar, rhetoric, ge-
ometry and the Holy Scriptures. And in these perils he
was strengthened by a particular aid.

8. For as he was still meditating upon his purpose, he came to the dwelling of a holy and devout woman. He at first addressed her humbly, afterwards he began to exhort her, as far as lay in his power. As she saw the increasing strength of the youth she said: "I have gone forth to the strife as far as it lay in my power. Lo, twelve years have passed by, since I have been far from my home and have sought out this place of pilgrimage. With the aid of Christ, never since then have I engaged in secular matters; after putting my hand to the plough, I have not turned backward. And if the weakness of my sex had not prevented me, I would have crossed the sea and chosen a better place among strangers as my home. But you, glowing with the fire of youth, stay quietly on your native soil; out of weakness you lend your ear even against your own will, to the voice of the flesh, and think you can associate with the female sex without sin. But do you recall the wiles of Eve, Adam's fall, how Samson was deceived by Delilah, how David was led to injustice by the beauty of Bathsheba, how the wise Solomon was ensnared by the love of a woman? Away, O youth! away! flee from corruption into which, as you know, many have fallen. Forsake the path which leads to the gates of hell."

The youth, trembling at these words, which were

such as to terrify a youth, thanked her for her reproaches, took leave of his companions and set out. His mother in anguish begged him not to leave her. But he said: "Hast thou not heard, 'He that loveth father or mother more than me is not worthy of me?'" He begged his mother, who placed herself in his way and held the door, to let him go. Weeping and stretched upon the floor, she said she would not permit it. Then he stepped across the threshold and asked his mother not to give way to her grief; she would never see him again in this life, but wherever the way of salvation led him, there he would go.

9. When he left behind him his native place, called by the inhabitants Lagener (Leinster, in Ireland), he betook himself to a holy man named Senilis, who at this time was distinguished among his countrymen for his unusual piety and knowledge of the Holy Scriptures. And when the holy man saw that St. Columban had great ability, he instructed him in the knowledge of all the Holy Scriptures. Nevertheless, as was usual, the master attempted to draw out the pupils under false pretences, in order that he might learn their dispositions, either the glowing excess of the senses, or the torpor induced by slothfulness. He began to inquire into Columban's disposition by difficult questions. But the latter tremblingly, nevertheless wisely, in order not to appear disobedient, nor touched by the vice of the love of vainglory, obeyed his master, and explained in turn all the objections that were made, mindful of that saying of the Psalmist, "Open thy mouth wide and I will fill it." Thus Columban collected such treasures of holy wisdom in his breast that he could, even as a youth, expound the Psalter in fitting language and could make many other extracts worthy to be sung, and instructive to read.

Then he endeavoured to enter a society of monks, and went to the monastery of Banchor (in the County of Ulster, in Ireland). The abbot, the holy Comgall, renowned for his virtues, was a faithful father to his monks and was held in high esteem for the fervour of his faith and the order and discipline which he preserved. Here Columban gave himself entirely to fasting and prayer, to bearing the easy yoke of Christ, to mortifying the flesh, to taking the cross upon himself and following Christ, in order that he who was to be a teacher of others might show the learning, which he taught, more fruitfully by his own example in mortifying his own body; and that he who was to instruct others might first instruct himself.

After he had been many years in the cloister he longed to go into the strange lands, in obedience to the command which the Lord gave Abraham: "Get thee out of thy country, and from thy kindred, and from thy father's house, into a land that I will show thee." Accordingly he confessed to the venerable father, Comgall, the burning desire of his heart and the longing enkindled by the fire of the Lord, concerning which the Lord says: "I am come to send fire on the earth; and what will I, if it be already kindled?" (Luke xii., 49. I have followed the King James version for the translation. The Vulgate, which is quoted here, reads *quem volo ut ardeat.*). But he did not receive the answer which he wished, for it was hard for Comgall to bear the loss of so great a comfort. At length, however, the latter began to conquer himself and to think that he ought not to consider his own need more than the necessities of others. Nor was it done without the will of the Almighty, who had educated His novice for future strifes, in order that He might win glorious triumphs from his victory and secure joyful victories from the phalanxes of slaughtered enemies.

The abbot accordingly called St. Columban, and although sorrowful, he considered the good of others before his own good, and bestowed upon him the bond of peace, the strength of solace and companions who were known for their piety.

10. Having collected a band of brethren, St. Columban asked the prayers of all, that he might be assisted in his coming journey, and that he might have their pious aid. So he started out in the twentieth (more probably thirtieth; the manuscripts differ) year of his life, and under the guidance of Christ went to the seashore with twelve companions. Here they waited to see if the mercy of the Almighty would allow their purpose to succeed, and learned that the spirit of the all-merciful Judge was with them. So they embarked, and began the dangerous journey across the channel and sailed quickly with a smooth sea and favourable wind to the coast of Brittany. Here they rested for a while to recover their strength and discussed their plans anxiously, until finally they decided to enter the land of Gaul. They wanted zealously and shrewdly to inquire into the disposition of the inhabitants in order to remain longer if they found they could sow the seeds of salvation; or in case they found the hearts of the people in darkness, go on to the nearest nations.

11. Accordingly, they left Brittany and proceeded into the Gallic lands. At that time, either because of the numerous enemies from without, or on account of the carelessness of the bishops, the Christian faith had almost departed from that country. The creed alone remained. But the saving grace of penance and the longing to root out the lusts of the flesh were to be found only in a few. Everywhere that he went the noble man preached the Gospel. And it pleased the people because his teaching was adorned by eloquence and enforced by examples of virtue.

So great was his humility and that of his followers, that just as the children of this world seek honour and authority, so they on the contrary vied with one another in the practice of humility, mindful of that saying: "He that humbleth himself shall be exalted," and of the text in Isaiah: "But to this man will I look, even to him that is poor and of a contrite spirit, and trembleth at my word." Such piety and love dwelt in them all, that for them there was only one will and one renunciation.

Modesty and moderation, meekness and mildness adorned them all in equal measure. The evils of sloth and dissension were banished. Pride and haughtiness were expiated by severe punishments. Scorn and envy were driven out by faithful diligence. So great was the might of their patience, love and mildness that no one could doubt that the God of mercy dwelt among them. If they found that one among them was in error, they strove in common, with equal right, to restrain the sinner by their reproaches. They had everything in common. If anyone claimed anything as his own, he was shut out from association with the others and punished by penances. No one dared to return evil for evil, or let fall a harsh word; so that people must have believed that an angelic life was being lived by mortal men. The holy man was reverenced with so great gratitude that where he remained for a time in a house, all hearts were resolved to practice the faith more strictly.

12.   Finally, the reports about Columban spread to the court of king Sigibert, who at this time ruled with honour over the two Frankish kingdoms of Austrasia and Burgundy. (Wrong; Sigibert died in 575, and was king only of Austrasia).   The name of the Franks was held in honour above that of any of the other inhabitants of Gaul.   When the holy man with his companions appeared before the king, the greatness of his learning caused him to stand high in the favour of the king and court.   Finally, the king begged him to remain in Gallic territory, not to go to other peoples and leave him; everything that he wished should be done.   Then he replied to the king that he did not wish to be enriched with the treasures of others, but as far as he was not hindered by the weakness of the flesh to follow the command of the Gospel: "Whosoever will come after me, let him deny himself and take up his cross and follow me."

Then the king answered and said: "If you wish to take the cross of Christ upon you and follow Him, seek the quiet of a hermitage.   Only be careful, for the increase of your own reward and for our spiritual good, to remain in our kingdom and not to go to the neighbouring peoples."   As the choice was left to him in this manner, he followed the king's advice and chose for himself a hermitage. At that time there was a great wilderness called *Vogasus* (the Vosges), in which there was a castle, which had long been in ruins, and which had been called for ages *Anagrates* (Anegray). When the holy man came to that place, he settled there with his followers, in spite of the entire loneliness, the wilderness and the rocks, mindful of the proverb that, "Man shall not live by bread alone," but shall have sufficient food from the bread of life and shall never hunger.

13. While the man of God was in that place with his companions, one of the brethren, either as a test or because of some sin, began to be chastised by a violent fever. Since they had no food except such as the barks and herbs furnished, they began with one mind to desire that all should give themselves up to prayer and fasting for the sake of the welfare of their sick brother. Having now fasted for three days and having nothing to refresh their wearied bodies, suddenly they saw a certain man standing before their gate with horses loaded and a supply of bread and condiments. He said that he had been led by a sudden impulse of his heart to bear aid from his own substance to those who were, for Christ's sake, suffering from so great poverty in the wilderness. Therefore, having presented to the man of God what he had brought, he began to ask earnestly that the holy man should pray to God on behalf of his wife, who for a whole year had been burning with so violent a fever that it now seemed impossible that she could be restored to health. As he made his request with an humble and contrite heart, the man of God was unwilling to deny him any comfort, and having called together the brethren he invoked the mercy of God on behalf of that woman. When he and his companions had completed their prayer, the woman who had been

in such imminent peril of death, was immediately restored to her health. When her husband had received
the benediction from the man of God and had returned
home, he found his wife sitting there. He questioned
her as to the time when the fever left her and learned
that she had been healed at the very hour when the man
of God had prayed to the Lord on her behalf.

14. Therefore, after a brief space of time in which they piously endeavoured to propitiate Christ and to atone for their evil thoughts, through mortification of the flesh and extreme fasting, they mortified their members to the glory of God, and desired to preserve the inviolate state of their religion. By their extreme severities every lust of the flesh was expelled, so that the plunderer and robber of all virtues fled. Nine days had already passed in which the man of God and his companions had taken no other food than the bark of trees and the roots of herbs. But the compassion of the divine virtue tempered the bitterness of the food. A certain abbot, named Carantoc, who ruled over a monastery of which the name was *Salicis,* was warned by a vision that he should bear the necessities of life to God's servant Columban, dwelling in the wilderness. Therefore, Caramtoc rising called his cellarer, Marculf by name, and told him what had happened. The latter replied, "Do as you have been told." Caramtoc therefore ordered Marculf to go and prepare everything that he could, to carry to St. Columban. Marculf, accordingly, having loaded his wagons started out. But when the hour of darkness came on, he sought in vain for a way to continue his journey. Nevertheless, he thought that if the command was from God, the power of the

Commander would show the way to the horses, if they were left to their own guidance. Wonderful power! The horses, advancing, followed an unknown road and in a direct course proceeded to Anegray to the doors of St. Columban; Marculf amazed followed the tracks of the horses, came to the man of God and presented what he had brought. The latter returned thanks to his Creator because He did not neglect to prepare a table for his servants in the wilderness. Therefore, having received a benediction from him, Marculf returned by the path by which he had come and disclosed to all what had happened. Then crowds of people and throngs of the infirm began to crowd around St. Columban in order that they might recover their health and in order to seek aid in all their infirmities. When he was unable to rid himself of their importunities, obeying the petitions and prayers of all, through his prayers and relying upon the divine aid, he healed the infirmities of all who came to him.

15. While the holy man was wandering through the dark woods and was carrying on his shoulder a book of Holy Scripture, he happened to be meditating. And suddenly the thought came into his mind which he would prefer to suffer, injuries from men or to be exposed to the rage of wild beasts. While he thought earnestly, frequently signing his forehead with the sign of the cross and praying, he decided that it was better to suffer from the ferocity of wild beasts, without any sin on their part, than from the madness of men who would lose their souls. And while he was turning this over in his mind, he perceived twelve wolves approaching and standing on the right and on the left, while he was in the middle. He stood still and said: "Oh, God, come to my aid. Oh, lord, hasten to aid me!" They came nearer and seized his clothing. As he stood firm they left him unterrified and wandered off into the woods. Having passed through this temptation in safety, he continued his course through the woods. And before he had gone far he heard the voices of many Suevi, wandering in the hidden paths. At this time they were robbing in those places. And so at length by his firmness having dismissed the temptation, he escaped the misfortune. But he did not know clearly whether this was some of the devil's deceit or whether

it had actually happened.

At another time he withdrew from his cell and entering the wilderness by a longer road he found an immense cliff with precipitous sides and rocky paths difficult for men. There he perceived a hollow in the rock. Entering to explore its hidden recesses he found in the interior of the cave the home of a bear, and the bear itself. He ordered the beast to depart and not to return to that place again. The beast mercifully went, nor did she dare to return again. The place was distant from Anegray seven miles more or less.

16. At one time he was living alone in that hollow rock, separated from the society of others and, as was his custom, dwelling in hidden places or more remotely in the wilderness, so that when the feasts of the Lord or saints' days came, he might, with his mind wholly free from disquieting cares, devote himself to prayer, and might be ready for every religious thought. He was so attenuated by fasting that he scarcely seemed alive. Nor did he eat anything except a small measure of the herbs of the field, or of the little apples which that wilderness produces and which are commonly called *bolluca*. His drink was water. And as he was always occupied with other cares, he could not get this regularly; at least during the time when he was performing his vows.

A little boy named Domoalis was in his service. This boy went alone to tell the father when certain events happened at the monastery and to carry back his directions to the brethren. When this boy had remained for several days in the hollow of this lofty rock, which was difficult of approach from all directions, he began to complain because he could not get water quickly. It tired his knees to bring it with so great labour through the difficult mountain paths. Columban said to him: "My son, get to work; make a little hole in the back of the rock. Remember the Lord produced streams of water from a rock for the people of Israel." He obeyed and attempted to make a hole in the rock. The holy man immediately fell upon his knees and prayed to God that He would aid him in his need. At length his prayers were heard; great power came to him, piously praying. And soon the fountain of water began to flow regularly and it remains to this day.

And not undeservedly has the merciful Lord granted the prayers if His saints, who on account of His commands have crucified their own wills, and who have so great faith that they do not doubt that they will obtain what they demand from His mercy. Because He has promised: "If ye have faith as a grain of mustard seed, ye shall say unto this mountain, remove hence to yonder place; and it shall remove; and nothing shall be impossible unto you." And elsewhere: "What things soever you desire, when ye pray, believe that ye receive them, and ye shall have them."

17. As the number of monks increased greatly, he sought in the same wilderness a better location for a convent. He found a place formerly strongly fortified, which was situated about eight miles from the first abode, and which had formerly been called Luxovium (Luxeuil in the department of Haute Saone). Here were baths constructed with unusual skill. A great number of stone idols, which in the old heathen times had been worshipped with horrible rites, stood in the forest near at hand. Here then the excellent man began to build a monastery. At the news of this people streamed in from all directions in order to consecrate themselves to the practice of religion, so that the large number of monks scarcely had sufficient room. The children of the nobles from all directions strove to come thither; despising the spurned trappings of the world and the pomp of present wealth, they sought eternal rewards. Columban perceived that the people were rushing in from all directions to the remedy of penance, and that the walls of one monastery could with difficulty hold so great a throng of converts. Although they were of one purpose and heart, yet one monastery was insufficient for the abode of so great a number. Accordingly he sought out another spot especially remarkable for its bountiful supply of water and founded a second convent

to which he gave the name *Fontanas* (Fountaines). In this he placed men whose piety could not be doubted. After he had settled the bands of monks in these places, he stayed alternately at the two convents, and full of the Holy Ghost, he established the rule which they were to follow. From this rule the prudent reader or listener may learn the extent and character of the holy man's learning. (The rule can be found in Migne, Patrilogiae, vol. lxxx).

18. At that time a brother, named Antierin, asked to be allowed to make a pilgrimage into Ireland. Columban said, "Let us go into the wilderness and try to learn the will of God, whether you ought to go on the journey as you desire or remain in the assembly of the brethren." Accordingly they went forth and took with them a third youth, named Somarius, who is still alive. They went to the place in the wilderness that had been fixed upon, taking with them only a single loaf. When twelve days had passed, and nothing remained from the fragments of bread, and the time for breaking their fast was approaching, they were commanded by the father to go through the rocky cliffs and down to the bottom of the valleys and to bring back whatever they found that was suitable for food.

They went joyfully through the sloping valleys, down to the Moselle and found some fishes which had been caught previously by fishermen and were floating about on the water. Approaching, they found five large fishes, and taking three, which were alive, they carried them back to the father. But he said, "Why did you not bring five?" They replied, "We found two dead, so we left them." But he said, "You shall not eat of these until you bring those which you left." They, struck with wonder at the fullness of the divine grace,

34

traversed again their dangerous path and chid themselves for leaving the manna which they had found.
Afterwards they were ordered to cook the food. For,
filled with the Holy Ghost, the father knew that the
food had been prepared for himself by God.

19. At another time he was staying in the same wilderness, but not in the same place. Fifty days had already elapsed and only one of the brethren named Gall was with him. Columban commanded Gall to go to the Brusch and catch fish. The latter went, took his boat and went to the Oignon river. After he had gotten there, and had thrown his net into the water he saw a great number of fishes coming. But they were not caught in the net, and went off again as if they had struck a wall. After working there all day and not being able to catch a fish, he returned and told the father that his labour had been in vain. The latter chid him for his disobedience in not going to the right place. Finally he said, "Go quickly to the place that you were ordered to try." Gall went accordingly, placed his net in the water, and it was filled with so great a number of fishes, that he could scarcely draw it.

20. At another time he was staying in the hollow of the rock mentioned above, from which he had expelled the bear, and for a long time he had been mortifying the flesh with prayer and fasting. By a revelation he learned that the brethren, who were near Luxeuil, were suffering from various diseases and only enough remained to care for the sick. Leaving his den, he went to Luxeuil. When he saw the afflicted, he commanded them all to rise and to thresh out the harvest on the threshing ground. Then those whose consciences were kindled by the fire of obedience arose and going to the threshing-place, attempted, full of faith, to thresh out the grain on the ground. The father seeing that they were full of faith and the grace of obedience, said, "Cease and rest your limbs, weakened by sickness." They obeyed, wondering at their recovery, for no trace of the diseases remained; and they prepared the tables as he commanded, that all might be strengthened by a joyful banquet. Then Columban chid the disobedient, showed them the inadequacy of their faith and announced the long continuance of their illness. Wonderful revenge! For the disobedient were so ill for an entire year that they barely escaped death. They accomplished the full measure of penance, from the time when they were disobedient.

21. Meanwhile the time had come for gathering the crops into the storehouses, but the violent winds did not cease to pile up clouds; nevertheless it was urgently necessary to gather the crops so that the ears of grain should not rot upon the stalks. The man of God was at the monastery of Fontaines, where a new field had yielded a very rich crop. Violent blasts piled up the rain-clouds, and the heavens did not cease to pour down the rain upon the earth. The man of God considered anxiously what he ought to do. Faith strengthened his mind and taught him how to command the fitting thing. He summoned all and ordered them to reap the crop. They wondered at the Father's command and no one understood his purpose. All came with their reaping hooks to cut the grain in the midst of the rain and watched to see what the father would do. He placed at the four corners of the field, four very religious men, Comininus, Eunocus and Equanacus, who were Scots, and the fourth Gurganus, a Briton. Having arranged them, he himself with the others cut the grain in the middle. Wonderful virtue! The shower fled from the grain and the rain was scattered in every direction. The warm sun poured down upon those who were reaping in the middle and a strong warm wind blew as long as they heaped up the grain. Faith and

prayer were of so great merit that the rain was driven off and they had sunshine in the midst of the storms.

22.   At that time there was a duke named Waldalen, who ruled over the people between the Alps and the Jura.   He had no children; in order that, as Juvencus says of Zacariah and Elizebeth, "the gift might be more welcome to those who had already given up hope."   He with his wife Flavia, who was noble both by her family and by her disposition, came from the town of Besançon to St. Columban.   Both of them begged of him that he would pray to the Lord on their behalf, for they had great wealth, but no son to whom they could leave it after their death.   The holy man said to them: "If you will promise to consecrate His gift to the Lord and will give me the child so that I can raise him from the baptismal font, I will invoke the Lord's mercy for you that you may have not only the one you consecrate to the Lord, but as many more as you desire."   Joyfully they promised what he wished, asking only that he would not cease to implore God to have mercy upon them.   The man of God promised that they should soon have what they wished, only they must not desire to break the compact.

Wonderful to relate! hardly had they returned home when the wife felt that she had conceived.   When she had borne a son, she brought him to the holy man and returned thanks to God, who had heard the prayers of

His servants. Columban consecrated the child to the Lord, raised him from the font and, naming him Donatus, gave him back to his mother to be nursed. Later on, the child was educated in the monastery and taught wisdom. He became Bishop of Besançon, which he still is. Out of love for St. Columban he founded a monastery under Columban's rule. From an ancient structure there it was named *Palatium*.

God fulfilled the promise made by His servant and gave to Waldalen a second son named Ramelen, distinguished for his nobility and wisdom. This son, after Waldalen's death, succeeded to his office, and although a layman he was truly filled with the fear of God. For he, too, out of love for the holy man, founded under his rule a monastery in the Jura mountains on the *Visona* River, and placed Siagrius there as abbot. The Lord added to His previous gifts two daughters, who were noble and perfect in the fear of Christ. After the death of her husband Flavia founded a nunnery in Besançon, gave it full protection and collected many nuns together. The grace of the man of God was so strong in them, that, despising all the vain pomp of this life, they were zealous in the service of God.

23. If we try to include some things which may seem of little importance, the goodness of the Creator, who is equally merciful in very small matters and in great, who does not delay to turn his pitying ear to trifling details, just as in the very important matters He grants the desires of the suppliant, will be manifest to those who bawl envious detractions. For on a certain day when the excellent man of God had gone with the brethren to cut the harvest near Calmem, which is called Baniaritia, and they were cutting the crop, while the south wind blew, one of them, named Theudegisil, happened to cut his finger with a sickle, and the finger hung by only a small strip of skin. The man of God seeing Theudegisil standing apart, commanded him to continue the work with his companions. But the latter told the reason for his actions. Columban hastened to him, and with his own saliva restored the wounded finger to its former health. Then he ordered Theudegisil to make haste and put forth more strength. The latter who had grieved for a long time over his cut finger, joyfully began to work doubly hard and to press on before the others in cutting the grain. Theudegisil himself, told us of this and showed his finger. A similar thing happened on another occasion at the monastery of Luxeuil.

24. For a parish priest, named Winnoe, the father of Babolen, who is now abbot of Bobbio, went to St. Columban. The latter was in the forest with the brethren, getting a supply of wood. When Winnoe arrived, and was watching with wonder how they split the trunk of an oak so easily with their mallet and wedges, one of the latter flying from the trunk cut him in the middle of his forehead, so that great waves of blood ran from his veins. Columban, the man of God, seeing the blood flowing, and the bone uncovered, immediately fell on the ground in prayer, then rising healed the wound with his saliva, so that hardly a sign of a scar remained.

25. On another occasion when St. Columban had come to dine at the monastery of Luxeuil, he laid his gloves, which the Gauls call *Wanti,* and which he was accustomed to wear when working, on a stone before the door of the refectory. Soon, in the quiet, a thievish raven flew up and carried off one of the gloves in its beak. After the meal, the man of God went out and looked for his gloves. When all were enquiring who had taken them, the holy man said, "There is no one who would venture to touch anything without permission, except the bird which was sent out by Noah and did not return to the ark." And, he added, that the raven would not be able to feed its young if it did not quickly bring back the stolen object. While the brethren were looking, the raven flew into their midst and brought back in its beak the object which it had basely stolen. Nor did it attempt to fly away, but forgetful of its wild nature, humbly in the sight of all, awaited its punishment. The holy man commanded it to go. Oh! wonderful power of the eternal Judge who grants such power to His servants that they are glorified both by honours from men and by the obedience of birds! (Grote says this miracle "is exactly in the character of the Homeric and Hesiodic age." See his interesting remarks in History of Greece, vol. 1, p.473, note, [Ed. New York, 1865]).

26. Another miracle was wrought by St. Columban and his cellarer, which I will relate. When the meal-time came, and the latter was ready to serve out the beer (which is boiled down from the juice of corn or barley, and which is used in preference to other beverages by all the nations in the world – except the Scottish and the barbarous nations who inhabit the ocean – that is, in Gaul, Brittany, Ireland, Germany and the other nations who do not deviate from the customs of the above) he carried to the cellar a jar, which was called a *tybrum,* and placed it before the vat in which the beer was. Having drawn the plug, he permitted the beer to flow into the jar. Another brother called him suddenly by the father's command. He, burning with the fire of obedience, forgot to put in the plug, which is called a *daciculum,* and, carrying it in his hand, hastened to the blessed man. After he had done what the man of God wished, he returned quickly to the cellar, thinking that nothing would be left in the vat from which the beer was running. But he saw the beer had run into the jar and not the least drop had fallen outside, so that you would have believed that the jar had doubled in size. Great was the merit of Columban commanding, great the obedience of the cellarer, that the Lord thus wished to avert sadness from both of

them, lest, if the zeal of either had diminished the substance of the brethren, both should go without needful
food; so the just Judge hastened to wash away the
faults of both, which had been committed by accident
and with the Lord's permission, but which each would
have asserted was due to his own remissness.

27. At that time the man of God, a lover of solitude, happened to be walking through the dense thickets of fruit-trees and found a bear ready to devour the body of a stag which wolves had killed, and the bear was licking up the blood. The man of God approached before it had eaten any of the flesh, and ordered it not to injure the hide which was needed for shoes. Then the beast, forgetting its ferocity, became gentle, and fawning and drooping its head left the body without a murmur, contrary to its custom. The man of God returning told this to the brethren, and ordered them to go and strip the hide from the body of the stag. When the brethren found the body they saw in the distance a great flock of birds of prey approaching, but these did not dare touch the body, on account of Columban's command. The brethren waited at a distance for a long time to see whether any beast or bird would attempt to take the forbidden food. They saw them come, attracted by the smell, stop at a distance, and, turning as if it were something deadly and fatal, fly swiftly away.

28. While Columban on another occasion was staying at Luxeuil, Winnoc, the priest whom we mentioned before, came to him and followed him wherever he went. They came to the storehouse in which the grain was kept. Winnoc, seeing and despising the smallness of the supply, said there was not enough to feed such a multitude, and chid him for his slothfulness in procuring food. St. Columban replied, "If men serve their Creator truly they will never feel need, for as the Psalmist makes known, 'I have not seen the righteous forsaken nor his seed begging their bread.' He, who satisfied five thousand men with five loaves, can very easily fill the storehouse with grain." While Winnoc stayed there that night, the storehouse was filled by the faith and prayers of the man of God. Winnoc, rising in the morning and passing by, unexpectedly saw the storehouse open and the custodian was standing before the door. He asked who had ordered this or what beasts of burden had brought the grain. The custodian replied, "It is not as you suppose. For see if the tracks of any animals are imprinted on the ground. The keys did not leave my person last night, but while the door was closed, the storehouse was filled with grain by the divine aid. Winnoc began to search carefully, with his eyes fixed on the ground, to seek for

traces of pack-animals. When he found nothing at all resembling these, he said, "The Lord is able to furnish a table for His servants in the wilderness."

A while after, Columban went to the monastery of Fontaines and found sixty brethren hoeing the ground and preparing the fields for the future crop. When he saw them breaking up the clods with great labour, he said, "May the Lord prepare for you a feast, my brethren." Hearing this the attendant said, "Father, believe me, we have only two loaves and a very little beer." Columban answered, "Go and bring those." The attendant went quickly and brought the two loaves and a little beer. Columban, raising his eyes to heaven, said, "Christ Jesus, only hope of the world, do Thou, who from five loaves satisfied five thousand men in the wilderness, multiply these loaves and this drink." Wonderful faith! All were satisfied and each one drank as much as he wished. The servant carried back twice as much in fragments and twice the amount of drink. And so he knew that faith is more deserving of the divine gifts than despair, which is wont to diminish even what one has.

29. When at one time the man of God was staying at Luxeuil, one of the brethren, who was also named Columban, was stricken with a fever and lying at the point of death, was awaiting instantly a happy release. When he wanted to draw his last breath, confident of the eternal reward which he had sought in his long service, he saw a man clothed in light coming to him, and saying, "I am not able now to free you from your body, because I am hindered by the prayers and tears of your father Columban." When the sick man heard this, sorrowfully, as if he had awakened from sleep, he began to call his attendant Theudegisil, whom we mentioned above, and said, "Go quickly and summon our father Columban to me." The attendant went swiftly, and, finding Columban weeping in the church, asked him to hasten to the sick man. Columban came quickly and asked him what he wanted. The latter told him, saying, "Why do you detain me by your prayers in this sorrowful world? For those are present, who would lead me away if they were not hindered by your tears and prayers. I beseech you, remove the obstacles which retain me that the celestial kingdom may open for me." Columban, struck with fear, made a signal that all should come. His joy lessened his grief at the loss of his holy companion. He gave the dying man the

body of Christ as a viaticum, and after the last kiss began the death-song. For they were of the same race and name and had left Ireland in the same company.

30. And do not wonder that the beasts and birds thus obeyed the command of the man of God. For we have learned from Chamnoald, royal chaplain at Laon, who was his attendant and disciple, that he has often seen Columban wandering about in the wilderness fasting and praying, and calling the wild beasts and birds. These came immediately at his command and he stroked them with his hand. The beasts and birds joyfully played, frisking about him, just as cats frisk about their mistresses. Chamnoald said he had often seen him call the litle animal, which men commonly name a *Squiruis,* from the tops of high trees and take it in his hand and put it on his neck and let it go into and come out from his bosom.

31. The fame of Columban had already penetrated into all parts of Gaul and Germany, and everyone was praising the venerable man. Theuderich too came often to him and humbly begged his prayers. For Theuderich had succeeded to the kingdom in the following manner: Sigibert had been murdered in the royal castle of Vitry (near Chalons), which is not far from Arras, at the instigation of his brother Chilperich, who was then living in Tournay and was being hunted to death by Sigibert. After the death of the latter, through the influence of his wife Brunhilda, the kingdom passed to his son Childebert (II). When the latter died in his youth (in 596), he was succeeded by his two sons, Theudebert and Theuderich, who ruled together with their grandmother Brunhilda. Austrasia went to Theudebert, Burgundy to Theuderich, who thought that he was fortunate in having St. Columban in his kingdom.

As he very often visited Columban, the holy man began to reprove him because he sinned with concubines, and did not satisfy himself with the comfort of a lawful wife, in order to beget royal children from an honoured queen, and not bastards by his concubines. After this reproof from Columban, the king promised to abstain from such sinful conduct. But the old serpent came to his grandmother Brunhilda, who was a second Jezebel, and aroused her pride against the holy man, because she saw that Theuderich was obedient to him. For she feared that her power and honour would be lessened if, after the expulsion of the concubines, a queen should rule the court.

32. St. Columban happened one day to go to Brunhilda, who was then living in *Brocariaca* (near Autun). As she saw him enter the court, she led to him the illegitimate sons of Theuderich. When St. Columban saw her, he asked what she wanted of him. Brunhilda answered, "These are the king's sons; give them thy blessing." He replied, "Know that these boys will never bear the royal sceptre, for they were begotten in sin." Enraged, she told the boys to go. When after this Columban left the court, a loud cracking noise was heard, the whole house trembled and everyone shook with fear. But that did not avail to check the wrath of the wretched woman.

From that time she began to persecute the neighbouring monasteries. She issued an order that none of the monks should be allowed to leave the lands of the monasteries, no one should receive them into other houses or give them any aid. When Columban saw that at the court all were arrayed against him, he hastened to *Spissia,* where the king was then staying, in order to subdue such defiance by his warnings. When he reached that place, about sunset, and it was announced to the king that Columban was there but would not enter the palace Theuderich said it would be better with due reverence to offer the needful services to the man of God, than to arouse the wrath of the Lord, by insulting His servant. Accordingly he ordered suitable food to be prepared in the royal kitchen and sent to the servant of God.

When the attendants came to Columban and, in accordance with the king's command, offered him food and drink prepared with royal magnificence, he asked what they meant by it. When they told him that it was sent by the king, he pushed it from him and said: "It is written, 'The most High is not pleased with the offerings of the wicked.' For it is not meet that the mouth of the servant of the Lord should be defiled by the food of him who shuts out the servant of God, not only from his own dwelling, but also from the dwellings of others." At these words all of the dishes broke into pieces, so that the wine and liquor ran out on the ground and the food was scattered here and there. Terrified, the servants announced this to the king. Full of anxiety, he, together with his grandmother, hastened to Columban early in the morning. Both begged him to forgive their past sins and promised amendment. With his fears quieted by this, Columban returned to his convent. But they failed to keep their promises, and very soon the persecutions were renewed with increased bitterness by the king, who continued in his

former sinful course. Then Columban sent him a letter
full of reproaches, and threatened him with the ban if
he did not amend his conduct.

33. Now Brunhilda began again to incite the king against Columban in every way; urged all the nobles and others at court to do the same, and influenced the bishops to attack Columban's faith and to abolish his monastic rule. She succeeded so fully that the holy man was obliged to answer for his faith or leave the country. The king, incited by Brunhilda, went to Luxeuil and accused Columban of violating the customs of the country and of not allowing all Christians to enter the interior of the monastery. To these accusations Columban answered, for he was unterrified and full of courage, that it was not his custom to allow laymen to enter the dwelling of the servant of God, but he had prepared a suitable place where all who came would be received. The king replied: "If you wish to enjoy any longer the gifts of our grace and favour, everyone in the future must be allowed free entrance everywhere." Columban answered: "If you dare to violate the monastic rule in any particular, I will not accept any gift or aid from you in the future. But if you come here to destroy the monasteries of the servant of God and to undermine their discipline and regulations, I tell you that your kingdom will be destroyed together with all your royal family." This the king afterward found to be true. In his audacity, he had already stepped into

the refectory; terrified by these words, he withdrew hastily.

But when Columban attacked him with bitter insults, Theuderich said: "You want me to honour you with the crown of martyrdom; do not believe that I am foolish enough to commit such a crime. But I will follow a wiser and more useful plan. Since you depart from the common customs, I will send you back to the home from which you came." At the same time the members of the court resolved unanimously that they would not put up with anyone who was unwilling to associate with everyone. But Columban said that he would not leave his monastery unless he was dragged out by force.

34. The king now withdrew, but left behind a nobleman named Baudulf. The latter drove the holy man out of his monastery and carried him to Besançon into banishment, until the king had determined what further action to take. While there Columban heard that the prison was full of condemned men awaiting the death penalty. The man of God hastened to them and, having entered the gate without opposition, he preached the word of God to the condemned. They promised him that if they were liberated they would amend their lives and would do penance for the crimes which they had committed. After this Columban commanded his attendant, whom we have mentioned above [ch. 16], to take in his hand the iron to which their feet were fettered, and to pull it. When the boy took hold of it and pulled, it broke into bits like the rotten trunk of a tree. Columban ordered the condemned to leave the prison now that their feet were free and, after preaching the Gospel to them, he washed their feet and dried them with a linen towel. Then he commanded them to go to the church and do penance for the crimes they had committed and to wash away their faults by their tears. They hastened thither and found the doors of the church fastened.

When the captain of the soldiers saw the fetters of

the condemned broken by Columban, through the power of God, and that only the empty prison remained, he started, although aroused from sleep, to follow the tracks of the condemned. The latter, seeing that the soldiers were coming after them and that the doors of the church were shut, hemmed in by the two-fold difficulty, reproached the man of God for having released them. But he, breathing anxiously, raised his face to heaven and prayed to the Lord that He would not permit those whom He had released from the iron by His strength, to be again delivered into the hands of the soldiers. Without delay, the goodness of the Creator opened the doors, which had been securely fastened, and disclosed a way of escape to those in peril. The condemned quickly entered the church. After their entrance the doors were shut without human hands, before the eyes of the soldiers, just as if a custodian with a key had unlocked them and then locked them again. Columban arriving with his followers and the captain coming up at the same time with his soldiers, found the doors shut. They sought the janitor, Aspasius by name, to get the key. When he came with they key and tried to open the doors he said he had never found them more tightly closed. Nor did anyone, after that, dare to do any injury to the condemned, whom the divine grace had liberated.

35.   As Columban now saw that he was not
watched at all and that no one did him any injury, (for
all saw that he was strong in the strength of the Lord
and therefore all refrained from injuring him, in order
not to be associated in guilt) one Sunday he climbed to
the top of the mountain.   Above, the lofty cliffs rise
perpendicularly into the heavens.   The mountain cut off
on all sides by the river Doubs, which surrounds it,
leaves no path open for travellers.   Columban waited
till noon to see whether anyone would prevent his returning to his monastery.   Then he took the road lead-
ing directly through the city.

When they heard of this, Brunhilda and Theuderich
were embittered still more.   They again ordered a band
of soldiers to carry off the man of God by violence and
to take him again to his former place of exile.   Accordingly the soldiers went with their captain and wandered through the precincts of the monastery, seeking
the man of God.   He was then in the vestibule of the
church reading a book.   They came repeatedly and
passed near him, so that some struck against him with
their feet and touched his garments with their garments, but did not see him because their eyes were
blinded.   And it was a most beautiful sight.   He, ex-
ulting, perceived that he was sought and was not

found. While he saw them, they did not see him sitting in the midst of them. The captain came and, looking through a window, saw the man of God sitting joyfully amid them and reading. Perceiving the power of God, he said: "Why do you go wandering about the vestibule of the church and do not find him? Your hearts are wholly filled with the madness of insanity; for you will not be able to find him whom the divine power conceals. Leave this undertaking and we will hasten to announce to the king that you could not find him." By this it was clearly shown that the captain of the soldiers had not come willingly to do injury to the man of God, and therefore had merited to see him.

36. They told the king. He, impelled by the madness of his wretched purpose, sent Count Bertarius and Baudulf, who was mentioned above, to the monastery. They finding the holy man in the church praying and singing psalms with all the brethren, said to him: "Oh man of God, we beg you to obey the king's orders and our own, and to return to the place whence you came to this land." But Columban answered, "I do not think it would be pleasing to my Creator if I should go back to the home which I left because of my love for Christ." When they saw that Columban would not obey them they withdrew. But they left behind several men of rough disposition and character.

Those who remained urged the man of God to have pity on them, since they had been perfidiously left behind to perform such a task, and to think of their peril. If they did not violently eject him they would be in danger of death. But he, as he had very often asserted, said he would not withdraw unless he were compelled to by violence. The men impelled by fear, since they were in immanent peril in either event, clung to the robe which he wore; others upon their knees besought him not to impute to them the guilt of so great a crime, since they were not following their own wishes, but obeying the commands of the king.

37. He finally decided to yield, in order not to imperil others, and departed amid universal sorrow and grief. Escorts were furnished him who were not to leave his side until they had conducted him to the boundary of the kingdom at Nantes. Ragamund was their leader. All the brethren followed, as if it were a funeral; for grief filled the hearts of all. The father in anxiety for the loss of so many members, raised his eyes to heaven, and said, "O Creator of the World, prepare for us a place where Thy people may worship Thee." Then he comforted the brethren, telling them to put their trust in the Lord and to give great praise to omnipotent God. This was not an injury to him or his followers, but an opportunity to increase the number of monks. Those who wished to follow him and had courage to bear all his sufferings might come. The others who wanted to remain in the monastery should do so, knowing that God would quickly avenge their injuries. But since the monks did not want to be deprived of the guardianship of their shepherd all resolved to go. But the king's servants declared that only those would be allowed to follow him who were his countrymen or who had come to him from Brittany; the others, by the king's command, were to remain in that place. When the father perceived that his follow-

ers were violently torn from him, his grief and that of his followers was increased. But he prayed to the Lord, the Comforter of all men, to take those into His own keeping, whom the king's violence tore from him. Among these was Eustasius, the scholar and servant of Columban, who was afterwards abbot in this very convent, of which his uncle, Mietius, bishop of Langres, had charge.

38.   So, twenty years after he had come to this place the holy man departed and went by way of Besançon and Autun to the fortress Cavalo.   On the way the king's master of horse wanted to kill him with a lance.   But the hand of God hindered it and lamed the man's hand, so that the lance fell on the ground at his feet and he himself seized by a supernatural power fell prone before Columban.   The latter, however, cared for him till the next morning and then sent him home healed.

39. From Cavalo he went to the river *Chora* (probably the Cure, a branch of the Jonne [Abel]) where he stayed in the house of a noble and pious lady, named Theudemanda, and healed twelve demoniacs who came to him. On the same day he went to the village of *Chora* where he healed five mad men. In Auxerre, which he next went to, he said to his companion, Ragamund, "Know that within three years Chlotar, whom you now despise, will be your lord." But he answered, "Why do you tell me such things, my lord?" The latter replied, "You will see what I have announced if you are still alive."

40. Then leaving Auxerre, Columban saw a youth possessed by a demon running swiftly toward him. This youth had run twenty miles with all his might. Seeing him, Columban waited until the man, wounded by the devil's art, should come. The latter fell at the feet of the man of God and was immediately cured by his prayers and visibly restored to health. Then with guards preceding and following, Columban came to the city of Nevers in order to go in a boat on the Loire to the coast of Brittany. When they had reached this point and had gotten into the boat with difficulty, one of the guards, taking an oar, struck one of them, who was named Lua, a most holy and devout man.

The man of God, seeing that one of his followers was struck in his presence, said: "Why, cruel man, do you add to my grief? Is not the guilt of the crime which you have committed sufficient for your destruction? Why do you appear merciless against the merciful? Why do you strike a wearied member of Christ? Why do you vent your wrath on the gentle? Remember that you will be punished by God in this place, where in your rage you have struck a member of Christ." The vengeance, soon following, executed the penalty inflicted by that sentence. For as the man was returning again and came to the same place to cross the river, struck by the divine vengeance, he was drowned. Why was it that the just Judge delayed the vengeance a little, unless it was that His saint might not be troubled by the sight of the man's punishment?

41.   From that place they went to the city of Orleans, where sorrowfully they rested for a time on the banks of the Loire in tents, for, by order of the king, they were forbidden to enter the churches. When finally their provisions gave out, they sent two men into the city to get food. One of these was Potentinus, who later on founded a convent in Armorica, near the city of Coutances (in the department of Manche), and who is still alive. When these men entered the city they found nothing, because the inhabitants, from fear of the king, did not dare to sell or give them anything, and they went back on the road by which they had entered the city. They met a Syrian woman in the street. When she saw them, she asked who they were. They explained the state of the case, and said that they were seeking food but had found nothing. She replied, "Come, my lords, to the house of your servant and take whatever you need. For I, too, am a stranger from the distant land of the Orient." They joyfully followed her to her house and sat down to rest until she brought what they sought. Her husband, who had long been blind, was sitting near them. When they asked him who he was, his wife replied, "My husband is from the same race of the Syrians that I am. As he is blind, I have led him about for many years." They said,

"If he should go to Columban, the servant of Christ, he would receive his sight through the holy man's prayers." The man having faith in the promised gift, regained his courage, rose and, led by his wife, followed them. They told Columban of the hospitality given to pilgrims. They had not finished their story before the blind man came and prayed the man of God to restore his sight by prayer.

Columban, seeing the man's faith, asked all to pray for the blind man, and after lying for a long time prone on the ground, he rose, touched the man's eyes with his hand and made the sign of the cross. The man received his longed-for sight. He rejoiced in his recovered sight, because it was fitting that he, whose soul had been lighted internally by hospitality, should not lack the external vision.

After that a band of mad men, whom demons tortured with savage fury, hastened to the man of God to be cured. Health was granted them by the lord; for all were healed by the man of God. The people of the city moved by these miracles supplied Columban with gifts secretly, because they did not dare to furnish anything openly on account of the guards, lest they should incur the wrath of the king. Thence Columban and his followers continued on their way.

42. And proceeding on the Loire, they came to the city of Tours. There the holy man begged the guards to stop and permit him to visit the grave of St. Martin. The guards refused, strove to go on quickly, urged the oarsmen to put forth their strength and pass swiftly by the harbour, and commanded the helmsman to keep the boat in mid-stream. St. Columban seeing this, raised his eyes sadly to heaven, grieving at being subjected to so great sorrow, and that he was not permitted to see the graves of the saints. In spite of all their efforts the boat stopped, as if anchored, as soon as it got opposite the harbour, and turned its bow to the landing-place. The guards seeing that they could not prevail, unwillingly allowed the boat to go where it would. In a wonderful manner it sped, as if winged, from mid-stream to the harbour, and entering this accomplished the wish of the man of God.

He, truly, gave thanks to the eternal King, who does not disdain to comply with the wishes of His servants. Landing, Columban went to the grave of St. Martin and spent the whole night there in prayer. In the morning he was invited by Leoparius, the bishop of the city, to break his fast. He accepted, especially for the sake of refreshing his brethren, and spent that day with the bishop. When he sat down at table with the bishop, at the hour of refection, and was asked why he was returning to his native land, he replied, "That dog Theuderich has driven me away from the brethren."

43. Then one of the guests, named Chrodowald, who was married to one of Theudebert's cousins, but who was a follower of Theuderich, replied in a humble voice to the man of God, "It is pleasanter to drink milk than wormwood," and declared that he would be faithful to king Theuderich, as he had sworn, so long as it was in his power. Columban said to him, "I know that you want to keep your oath of fidelity to king Theuderich, and you will be glad to take my message to your lord and friend, if you serve king Theuderich. Announce, therefore, to Theuderich that he and his children will die within three years, and his entire family will be exterminated by the Lord." "Why," said the man, "do you announce such tidings, O servant of God?" "I dare not conceal what the Lord has ordered me to reveal." All the inhabitants of Gaul saw this fulfilled later, and this confirmed what had been announced previously to Ragamund.

44. After the repast, the man of God returned to the boat and found his companions very sorrowful. On enquiring what had happened, he learned that what they had in the boat had been stolen in the night, and also the gold which he had not given to the poor. Having heard this, he returned to the grave of the holy confessor and complained that he had not watched by the relics of the saint in order that the latter should allow him and his followers to suffer loss. Immediately he who had stolen the bag of gold began to be tormented and tortured, and cried out that he had concealed the pieces of gold in this place and that. All his associates rushed to return all that had been stolen and prayed the man of God to pardon the great crime. This miracle struck such terror into all, that those who heard of it did not dare to touch anything which belonged to the man of God, believing that all was consecrated. After supplying him with food, Leoparius said farewell to St. Columban.

45. Joyfully then they went in the boat to the city of Nantes and there stopped for a short time. One day a beggar cried out before the door of the cell in which the man of God was meditating. Calling an attendant, Columban said; "Give the beggar some food." The attendant replied: "We have nothing except a very little meal." He asked: "How much have you?" The attendant replied that he thought he did not have more than a measure of meal. "Then give it all," he said, "and save nothing for the morrow." The servant obeyed and gave all to the beggar, reserving nothing for the common need.

Already the third day had dawned since they had been fasting, and had had scarcely anything except the grace of hope and faith, by which to refresh their exhausted limbs. Suddenly they heard the door open; when the doorkeeper asked why the ears of the brethren were troubled by the din, he who had opened the door said he had been sent by his mistress Procula. She said she had been divinely warned to send food to the man of God, Columban, and to his companions, who were staying near the city of Nantes. The man said the food would come immediately, and that he had been sent ahead to tell them to prepare receptacles to receive it. There were a hundred measures of wine, two hundred of grain, and a hundred of barley. The doorkeeper hastened to announce this to the father. But the latter said, very well, he knew it, and ordered that the brethren should come together to pray to the Lord in behalf of their benefactress, and at the same time to return thanks to their Creator who never fails to comfort His servants in every need; and after that they would receive the gifts.

Wonderful compassion of the Creator! He permits us to be in need, that He may show His mercy by giving to the needy. He permits us to be tempted, that by aiding us in our temptations He may turn the hearts of His servants more fully to Himself. He permits His followers to be cruelly tortured that they may delight more fully in restored health.

46.   Another equally noble and pious woman, named Doda, sent two hundred measures of corn, and a hundred of mixed grain. This caused very great shame to the bishop of that city, named Suffronius, from whom nothing could be obtained as a gift or even by exchange. While Columban remained there, a certain woman tormented by a demon came to him, together with her daughter who was also suffering from a severe disease. When he saw them, he prayed to the Lord for them; after they had been healed, he commanded them to return home.

47.   After this Suffronius, bishop of Nantes, and count Theudebald made preparations to send St. Columban to Ireland, in accordance with the king's orders.   But the man of God said: "If there is a ship here which is returning to Ireland, put my effects and my companions on it.   In the meantime I will go in my skiff down the Loire to the ocean.   They found a vessel which had brought Scottish wares and embarked all Columban's effects and companions.   When with a favourable wind the oarsmen were now rowing the vessel down to the ocean, a huge wave came and drove the vessel on shore.   It stuck fast on the land, and the water receding, remained quietly in the channel.   The bark remained high and dry for three days.   Then the captain of the vessel understood that he was detained in this manner on account of the effects and companions of the man of God, that he had taken on board.   He decided to disembark from the vessel all that belonged to Columban.   Immediately a wave came and bore the vessel out to the ocean.   Then all, filled with amazement, understood that God did not wish Columban to return home.

Accordingly he returned to the house in which he had formerly dwelt and no one opposed him; nay, rather, all aided the man of God with gifts and food, as far as lay in their power. Nor did he lack defence, because in all things he had the aid of the Creator, and He who keeps Israel under the shadow of His wings never slumbers. Thus truly He shows by granting all things to all men, that He wishes to be glorified by all in proportion to the greatness of his gifts.

48. Not long after this Columban went to Chlotar, Chilperic's son, who ruled in Neustria over the Franks who lived on the coast. Chlotar had already heard how the man of God had been persecuted by Brunhilda and Theuderich. He now received Columban as a veritable gift from heaven, and begged that he would remain in Neustria. Columban refused and said that he did not wish to remain there, either for the sake of increasing the extent of his pilgrimage, or for the sake of avoiding enmities. But he remained some time with the king, and called his attention to several abuses, such as could hardly fail to exist at a king's court. Chlotar promised to correct everything according to Columban's commands, for he zealously loved wisdom, and rejoiced in the blessing which he had secured.

In the meantime a strife arose between Theudebert and Theuderich over the boundaries of their kingdoms, and both sent to Chlotar to beg aid. The latter was disposed to aid one against the other, and asked Columban's advice. He, filled with the spirit of prophesy, answered that Chlotar ought not to unite with either, for within three years he would receive both kingdoms. Chlotar seeing that such things were prophesied by the man of God, aided neither, but full of faith awaited the promised time. Afterwards he triumphed victoriously.

49.   Afterwards, Columban asked Chlotar to aid him to go through Theudebert's territory, if possible, and over the Alps to Italy. He received escorts who were to conduct him to Theudebert, and entering upon his journey went to the city of Paris. When he arrived there, he met at the gate a man having an unclean spirit, who was raving and rending his garments, while babbling.   The latter addressed the man of God complainingly: "What are you doing in this place, O man of God?" From afar he had been crying out for a long time with his growling voice as he saw Columban, the man of God, approaching.   When the latter saw him, he said: "Depart, evil one, depart! Do not dare to possess any longer the body washed by Christ. Yield to the power of God, and invoked by the name of Christ." But when the devil resisted for a long time with savage and cruel strength, the man of God placed his hand on the man's ear and struck the man's tongue, and by the power of God commanded the devil to depart. Then rending the man with cruel violence so that bonds could scarcely restrain him, the devil, issuing forth amid great purging and vomiting, made such a stench that those who stood by believed that they could endure the fumes of sulphur more easily.

50. Then Columban went to the city of Meaux. There he was received with great joy by a nobleman Hagneric, who was a friend of Theudebert, a wise man, and a counsellor grateful to the king, and was fortified by nobility and wisdom. The latter promised that he would take care of Columban until the latter reached the court of Theudebert, and said it was not necessary to have the other companions who were sent by the king. He declined the aid of the others in order to keep the man of God with himself as long as he could, and in order that his house might be ennobled by the learning of the latter. Columban blessed his house and consecrated to the Lord his daughter Burgundofara, who was still a child, and of whom we shall speak later.

Thence he proceeded to Eussy on the river Marne. There he was received by a man named Antharius, whose wife was named Aiga. They had sons under ten years of age, whom the mother brought to the man of God to be blessed. He, seeing the faith of the mother, consecrated the little children with his blessing. They later, when they grew up, were held in high esteem, first by king Chlotar, afterwards by Dagobert. After they had obtained great glory in the world, they made haste, lest in the glory of this world they should lose the eternal. The elder. Ado, withdrew of his own accord and founded, under the rule of St. Columban, a monastery near Mt. Jura (the Monastery Jouarre near Meaux). The younger, Dado, founded, under the rule of the blessed man, a monastery near Brieg, on the little river Rébais.

So greatly did the man of God abound in faith, that whomever he consecrated, the last day found persevering in good works. And those whom he warned, rejoiced afterward that they had merited immunity. Nor did he, endued with so great strength, undeservedly obtain an increase of grace, who guided by his learning, was unwilling to deviate from the path of a just life.

51.   From that place Columban proceeded to
Theudebert, who received him joyfully. Many brethren
had already come to him from Luxeuil, whom he received as if they had been snatched from his enemy.
Now the king promised to seek out beautiful places,
suitable for God's servants, where they could preach to
the neighbouring people.   Columban declared, that if
the king was in earnest and would actively support him,
he would gladly remain there longer and try to sow the
seeds of faith in the hearts of the neighbouring peoples.
Theudebert commissioned him to choose a suitable
place, and, with the approval of all, he decided upon a
long-ruined city, which was in the German land not far
from the Rhine, and which was called *Brigantia*
(Bregenz).   But what the man of God did, as he was
ascending the Rhine in his boat, must not be passed
over in silence.

52 As they journeyed, they came to the city which was formerly called Maguntiacum (Mainz). The oarsmen who had been sent by the king to aid the man of God, told him they had friends in the city who would supply needful food; for already they had been long fasting. The man of God told them to go; but they did not find any. They returned, and in reply to the questions of the man of God said they had been unable to obtain anything from their friends. Then he said, "Let me go for a short time to my friend." They wondered how he had a friend there, where he had never been before. But he went to the church and, entering, threw himself on the pavement, and in a long prayer sought the protection of God, the source of all mercy. Immediately the bishop of the city went from his home to the church and, finding Columban, asked who he was. The latter said he was a pilgrim. The bishop answered: "If you need food, go to my house and take what you need." After thanking him and also the Creator who had inspired him, Columban hastened to the boat and directed that all the men, except one guard, should go and bring what they wished. But lest this should seem to anyone mere chance, that bishop was accustomed to protest that he had never before given food with so little thought. And he testified that he went to the

church that day by divine admonition, on account of the merit of the blessed Columban.

53. At length they arrived at the place designated, which did not wholly please Columban; but he decided to remain, in order to spread the faith among the people, who were Swabians. Once, as he was going through this country, he discovered that the natives were going to make a heathen offering. They had a large cask that they called a *Cupa,* and that held about twenty-six measures, filled with beer and set in their midst. On Columban's asking what they intended to do with it, they answered that they were making an offering to their God Wodan (whom others call Mercury). When he heard of this abomination, he breathed on the cask, and lo! it broke with a crash and fell in pieces so that all the beer ran out. Then it was clear that the devil had been concealed in the cask, and that through the earthly drink he had purposed to ensnare the souls of the participants. As the heathens saw that, they were amazed and said Columban had a strong breath, to split a well-bound cask in that manner. But he reproved them in the words of the Gospel, and commanded them to cease from such offerings and to go home. Many were converted then, by the preaching of the holy man, and turning to the learning and faith of Christ, were baptized by him. Others, who were already baptized but still lived in the heathenish unbelief,

like a good shepherd, he again led by his words to the faith and into the bosom of the church.

54. At that time Theuderich and Brunhilda were venting their wrath not only on Columban, but also on the holy Desiderius, bishop of Vienne. After they had driven the latter into banishment and had done him much evil, they crowned him at last with a glorious martyr's death. By his deeds, which have been narrated, and by his great adversities he deserved to have a glorious triumph near the Lord.

In the meantime Columban and his companions experienced a time of great need near the city of Bregenz. But although they were without food, they were bold and unterrified in their faith, so that they obtained food from the Lord. After their bodies had been exhausted by three days of fasting, they found so great an abundance of birds, --just as the quails formerly covered the camp of the children of Israel, --that the whole country near there was filled with birds. The man of God knew that this food had been scattered on the ground for his own safety and that of his brethren, and that the birds had come only because he was there. He ordered his followers first to render grateful praises to the Creator, and then to take the birds as food. And it was a wonderful and stupendous miracle; for the birds were seized according to the father's commands and did not attempt to fly away. The manna of birds remained for three days. On the fourth day, a priest from an adjacent city, warned by divine inspiration, sent a supply of grain to St. Columban. When the supply of grain arrived, the Omnipotent, who had furnished the winged food to those in want, immediately commanded the phalanxes of birds to depart. We learned this from Eustasius, who was present with the others, under the command of the servant of God. He said that no one of them remembered ever having seen birds of such a kind before; and the food was of so pleasant savor that it surpassed royal viands. Oh, wonderful gift of divine mercy! When earthly food was wanting to the servants of Christ, celestial was furnished; as was said of Israel: "He gave to them of the corn of heaven;" when earthly food was brought, the celestial which had been mercifully granted was taken away.

55. Then Columban was weakening his body by fasting, under a cliff in the wilderness, and he had no food except the apples of the country, which we have mentioned above. A fierce bear of great voracity came and began to lick off the necessary food and carry the apples away in its mouth. When the meal-time came, Columban directed Chagnoald, his servant, to bring the usual quantity of apples. The latter went and saw the bear wandering about among the fruit-trees and bushes and licking off the apples. He returned hastily and told the father, who commanded him to go and set aside a part of the fruit-trees for food for the bear and order it to leave the others for himself. Chagnoald went in obedience to the command, and dividing with his staff the trees and bushes which bore the apples, he, in accordance with Columban's command, set aside the part that the bear should eat, and the other part that it should leave for the use of the man of God. Wonderful obedience of the bear! It did not venture at all to take food from the prohibited part but, as long as the man of God remained in that place, sought food only from the trees that had been assigned to it.

56. Once Columban thought of going to the land of the Wends, who are also called Slavs, in order to illuminate their darkened minds with the light of the Gospel, and to open the way of truth to those who had always wandered in error. When he purposed to make his vows, the angel of the Lord appeared to him in a vision, and showed him in a little circle the structure of the world, just as the circle of the universe is usually drawn with a pen in a book. "You perceive," the angel said, "how much remains set apart of the whole world. Go to the right or the left where you will, that you may enjoy the fruits of your labours." Therefore Columban remained where he was, until the way to Italy opened before him.

57.   In the meantime a compact of peace which
Theuderich and Theudebert had made was broken, and
each one, priding himself on the strength of his followers, endeavoured to kill the other.   Then Columban
went to king Theudebert and demanded that he should
resign his kingdom and enter a monastery, in order not
to lose both earthly crown and everlasting life.   The
king and his companions laughed; they had never heard
of a Merovingian on the throne, who had voluntarily
given up everything and become a monk.   But
Columban said, if the king was not willing voluntarily
to undertake the honour of the priestly office, he would
soon be compelled to do it against his will.   After these
words, the holy man returned to his cell; but his
prophecy was soon verified by events.   Theuderich immediately advanced against Theudebert, defeated him
near Zülpich, and pursued him with a great army.
Theudebert gathered new forces and a second battle
was fought near Zülpich.   Many fell on both sides, but
Theudebert was finally defeated and fled.

At that time the man of God was staying in the
wilderness, having only one attendant, Chagnoald.   At
the hour when the battle near Zülpich began, Columban
was sitting on the trunk of a rotten oak, reading a
book.   Suddenly he was overcome by sleep and saw

what was taking place between the two kings. Soon after he aroused, and calling his attendant, told him of the bloody battle, grieving at the loss of so much human blood. His attendant said with rash presumption: "My father, aid Theudebert with your prayers, so that he may defeat the common enemy, Theuderich." Columban answered: "Your advice is foolish and irreligious, for God, who commanded us to pray for our enemies has not so willed. The just Judge has already determined what He wills concerning them." The attendant afterwards enquired and found that the battle had taken place on that day and at that hour, just as the man of God had revealed to him.

Theuderich pursued Theudebert, and the latter was captured by the treachery of his followers and sent to his grandmother, Brunhilda. She, in her fury, because she was on Theuderich's side, shut him up in a monastery, but after a few days she mercilessly had him murdered.

58. Not long after this Theuderich, struck by the hand of the Lord, perished in a conflagration in the city of Metz. Brunhilda then placed the crown on the head of his son Sigibert. But Chlotar thought of Columban's prophecy and gathered together an army to reconquer the land which belonged to him. Sigibert with his troops advanced to attack him, but was captured, together with his five brothers and great grandmother Brunhilda, by Chlotar. The latter had the boys killed, one by one, but Brunhilda he had first placed on a camel in mockery and so exhibited to all her enemies round about; then she was bound to the tails of wild horses and thus perished wretchedly. As the whole family of Theuderich was now exterminated, Chlotar ruled alone over the three kingdoms (Neustria, Austrasia and Burgundy), and Columban's prophecy had been literally fulfilled. For one of the kings and his whole family had been entirely exterminated within three years; the second had been made a clerk by violence; the third was the possessor and ruler of all the kingdoms.

59. When Columban saw that Theudebert had been conquered by Theuderich, as we said above, he left Gaul and Germany and went to Italy. There he was received with honour by Agilulf, king of the Lombards. The latter granted him the privilege of settling in Italy wherever he pleased; and he did so, by God's direction. During his stay in Milan, he resolved to attack the errors of the heretics, that is, the Arian perfidy, which he wanted to cut out and exterminate with the cauterizing knife of the Scriptures. And he composed an excellent and learned work against them.

60. At that time a man named Jocundus appeared before the king and announced that he knew of a church of the holy apostle Peter, in a lonely spot in the Apennines; the place had many advantages, it was unusually fertile, the water was full of fishes; it had long been called *Bobium* (Bobbio), from the brook that flowed by it. There was another river in the neighbourhood, by which Hannibal had once passed a winter and suffered the loss of a great number of men, horses and elephants. Thither Columban now went, and with all diligence restored to its old beauty the church which was already half in ruins.

In this restoration the wonderful power of the Lord was visible. For, when beams of fir were cut amid the precipitous cliffs or in the dense woods, or those cut elsewhere, fell into such places by accident, so that beasts of burden could not approach, the man of God going with two or three companions, as many as the steep paths furnished footing for, placed, in a wonderful manner, on his own and his companions' shoulders beams of immense weight, which thirty or forty men could scarcely carry on level ground; and where they had hardly been able to walk before, on account of the steepness of the paths, and had moved as if weighed down with burdens, they now walked easily and joyfully, bearing their burden. The man of God, seeing that he was receiving so great aid, urged his companions to finish joyfully the work which they had begun, and to remain in the wilderness with renewed courage, affirming that this was God's will. Therefore he restored the roof of the church and the ruined walls, and provided whatever else was necessary for a monastery.

61. During this time king Chlotar, when he saw that the words of Columban had been fulfilled, summoned Eustasius, who was then abbot of Luxeuil, and urged him to go with an escort of noblemen, whom Eustasius himself should select, to the holy Columban and beg the latter, wherever he might be, to come to Chlotar. Then the venerable disciple went to seek his master, and when he found the latter, he repeated Chlotar's words. But Columban declared, when he heard Chlotar's request, that he could not undertake the journey again. Eustasius he kept with himself for some time, warned him not to forget his own labours and work, to keep the band of brethren learned and obedient, to increase their numbers and educate them according to his instructions.

To the king he sent a letter full of good advice, and begged him to extend his royal protection and aid to the brethren at Luxeuil. The king received the letter joyfully, as a most pleasing gift and as a pledge of his compact with the man of god. Nor did he forget the latter's request, but showed his favour in every way to the cloister, gave it yearly revenues, increased its territory in every direction, where the venerable Eustasius desired, and aided its inmates in every way that he could. After a single year in his monastery of Bobbio,

Columban, the man of God, ended his devout life on the XI. day before the Kalends of December (November 1st., probably 615). If anyone wishes to learn of his activity, let him seek it in the saint's writings (reprinted in Migne, vol. 80). His remains are buried there (in Bobbio), where they have proved their virtues, by the aid of Christ. To Him be glory for ever and ever, world without end. Amen.

ALSO PUBLISHED BY LLANERCH:

THE LIFE OF CEOLFRID
BY AN ANONYMOUS MONK OF JARROW

THE LIFE OF ST. COLUMBA
BY ADAMNAN

THE LIFE OF ST. GALL
BY MAUD JOYNT

SYMBOLISM OF THE
CELTIC CROSS
BY DEREK BRYCE

NORTHUMBRIAN CROSSES
OF THE PRE-NORMAN AGE
BY W. G. COLLINGWOOD

FROM BOOKSELLERS.
For a complete list, write to LLANERCH PUBLISHERS,

Felinfach, Lampeter, Dyfed, SA48 8PJ.

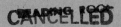